Deserters

20 exciting real cases

Phillips Tahuer

Ediciones Afrodita

Contents

Introduction

Throughout history, there have been times when borders have not only been dividing lines on a map but also barriers that separate ideological worlds, political realities, and personal conflicts. In that context, deserters break with the established order, renouncing their homeland and embracing a new reality, often with great risks and profound consequences. Whether due to political convictions, ideological reasons, or simply the need to survive, these individuals decided to leave their country, in many cases to join another that represented the opposite of what they had known.

"Deserters" is a journey through 20 famous cases that have marked modern history, where men and women have become protagonists of transcendental changes, either as traitors or as heroes, depending on the side from which you look at it. From high-ranking espionage officers who betrayed state secrets, to intellectuals and artists who fled oppression in search of freedom, these stories are testimonies of the internal and external struggles that can lead a person to cross not only physical but also moral boundaries.

This book explores not only the facts behind each defection but also the deep motivations that pushed these individuals to abandon their national loyalties.

What did they feel when they left behind the flag that flew over their lives? What are the pressures, fears, or ideals that can justify a betrayal in the eyes of some of the search for freedom for others? In each case, we will find not only a historical fact but a reflection of the tensions between the individual and the State, power and resistance, loyalty and freedom.

Through these stories, "Deserters" aims to offer a close look at the most difficult decisions that a human being can face, those that redefine their life and, in many cases, alter the course of history itself.

1. Kim Philby: The spy who betrayed his country in favor of the Soviet Union

Harold Adrian Russell Philby, better known as Kim Philby, was one of the most famous and controversial defectors of the 20th century. Born in 1912 in British India, he was educated at the prestigious Trinity College, Cambridge, where he formed relationships with a circle of friends who shared a Marxist-Leninist political vision, influenced by the turbulent times of the 1930s. Throughout his life, Kim Philby would be one of the most effective spies in the service of the Soviet Union, infiltrating the highest levels of the British intelligence services and playing a crucial role in the Cold War.

Philby was recruited by Soviet intelligence in the 1930s while posing as a fervent anti-communist. His apparent loyalty to the British Empire allowed him to join the United Kingdom's Secret Intelligence Service, MI6, in 1940. From within, Philby began providing valuable information to the Soviet Union about British and Allied operations during World War II and the Cold War.

During his rise, Philby managed to fill key roles within British intelligence, even rising to become the head of the section responsible for counterintelligence against the USSR. From that position, he was able to not only sabotage Western efforts to counter Soviet operations but also warn Moscow about double-dealing and covert operations that threatened the Kremlin.

Kim Philby was part of a group known as the Cambridge Circle; a spy network made up of five

Cambridge-educated men who secretly worked for the USSR. In addition to Philby, other prominent members of this circle included Guy Burgess, Donald Maclean, Anthony Blunt, and John Cairncross. These men shared an affinity for communism and saw in the Soviet Union a hope for global stability in the face of what they saw as the failings of Western capitalism.

What makes Philby especially unique is his ability to deceive both his peers and superiors for years, even after other members of the circle were unmasked. While Burgess and Maclean defected to the USSR in 1951, Philby was suspected but never formally indicted.

Kim Philby's motives for betraying his country were primarily ideological. In his youth, he was deeply influenced by Marxism and Leninism, seeing in the Soviet Union a viable alternative to the imperialist and capitalist systems of power that dominated the Western world. During the 1930s, amid the Great Depression and the rise of fascism in Europe, Philby concluded that Soviet communism was the only hope for humanity, a belief that stayed with him throughout his life.

His dedication to this cause led him to betray his country, friends, and colleagues, and to act as a key cog in the Soviet spy machine.

Philby's life began to unravel when, in 1963, suspicions about his double life became untenable. Although he had avoided being formally charged for years, a series of interrogations and new evidence left him vulnerable. That same year, while stationed in

Beirut as a press correspondent (a cover for his spy work), he received indications that the net was closing in on him.

On January 23, 1963, Philby disappeared from Beirut. He boarded a Soviet merchant ship that took him to Odessa (now in Ukraine), where he was welcomed as a hero. Despite his defection and his years of loyal service to the Soviet regime, Philby's life in the USSR was not entirely happy. Although he was treated with respect, he lived in relative isolation, with frequent bouts of alcoholism and longing for his former life in the United Kingdom.

Philby spent the rest of his life in the Soviet Union, where he was rewarded with an apartment and a stipend, though not the public recognition he had hoped for. He married Rufina Pukhova, his fourth wife, and lived a modest life, though not without personal and psychological strains.

Despite initial distrust by some Soviet quarters, Philby was decorated and held up as a propaganda piece for the success of Soviet espionage. He died in 1988 in Moscow, aged 76. In Russia, he is regarded as a hero, while in his homeland, the United Kingdom, he is seen as one of history's most notorious traitors.

Philby's case forever changed the dynamics of Cold War espionage. His defection and the revelation of his activities within MI6 generated a wave of paranoia in the British and American secret services, calling into question the reliability of their operatives. It also provided the Soviet Union with an invaluable strategic advantage for decades to come.

Kim Philby, the perfect spy, not only betrayed his country but left an indelible mark on the history of international espionage and the Cold War, becoming a character that continues to fascinate historians, writers, and analysts of the modern world.

2. Edward Snowden: The man who revealed America's system of mass surveillance

Edward Joseph Snowden, born on June 21, 1983, in Elizabeth City, North Carolina, is one of the most notorious defectors of the 21st century. A former contractor for the US National Security Agency (NSA), Snowden became a central figure in the debate over privacy, government surveillance, and national security when, in 2013, he revealed to the world the massive spying programs implemented by the US government and its allies. His leaks caused an earthquake in international politics and led him to seek refuge in Russia, where he has lived ever since.

Snowden grew up in a family with strong ties to the US government: his father worked in the Coast Guard and his mother in the federal judicial system. After trying to enlist in the military, Snowden entered the world of intelligence, working first for the CIA and then for the NSA as a contractor, through private companies such as Booz Allen Hamilton. His access to classified information allowed him to learn the details of large-scale surveillance programs that monitored global communications, including emails, phone calls, and internet activity.

In 2009, Snowden was assigned to a posting in Japan, and it was there that he began to seriously question the mass surveillance programs that the US government was carrying out. The PRISM program, which allowed the NSA to obtain user data from large technology companies such as Google, Facebook, and Apple, was one of the most troubling points for Snowden, as it involved a widespread invasion of the privacy of millions of people without their consent.

Snowden claimed that his decision to leak classified information to the press was driven by his moral principles and his belief that the world's citizens had a right to know that they were being massively monitored, not only by the US government, but by a global spy network that included close allies such as the United Kingdom, Australia, Canada, and New Zealand (known as the "Five Eyes" group).

For Snowden, the US government had overstepped the boundaries of national security, implementing a system of mass surveillance that violated the Fourth Amendment to the US Constitution, which protects against unreasonable searches and seizures. His motivations were not those of a typical defector who switches sides for ideological or political reasons but were driven by a deep sense of justice and human rights.

In May 2013, at the age of 29, Snowden left his job at the NSA and flew to Hong Kong, where he secretly met with journalists from The Guardian and The

Washington Post. Snowden gave these journalists a huge trove of classified documents that revealed the extent of the spying programs. Among the documents were information about XKeyscore, a tool used by the NSA to collect data on internet users globally, and Boundless Informant, a program that classified information collected by the NSA based on geographic location.

The first leaks were published in June 2013 and caused a global scandal. The documents revealed that the NSA was monitoring the communications of not only American citizens but also world leaders, companies, and foreign governments, including those of allied countries. The impact was immediate, with global leaders such as Angela Merkel expressing outrage at discovering that their communications were being spied on.

Following the leaks, Snowden became a hunted figure by the US government, accused of violating the Espionage Act of 1917 and stealing government property. From Hong Kong, Snowden attempted to travel to Latin America, seeking refuge in countries such as Ecuador and Venezuela, which had shown willingness to grant him asylum. However, in June 2013, his passport was revoked by the US government, leaving him stranded at Sheremetyevo Airport in Moscow.

After more than a month in the airport's transit area, Russia granted him temporary asylum for one year, which was renewed several times. In 2020, Snowden was granted permanent residency in Russia. Despite US efforts to extradite him, Russia has refused to hand him over, straining relations between the two countries.

Since he arrived in Russia, Snowden has kept a relatively low profile, although he has continued to participate in public debates about privacy and digital rights through online lectures, interviews, and his Twitter account. In 2019, he published his autobiography Permanent Record, in which he recounts his life, the leaks, and the motives behind his actions.

Snowden has lived in Moscow with his wife, Lindsay Mills, whom he secretly married in 2017. Despite being physically in Russia, Snowden has continued to denounce surveillance and defend privacy from a global perspective, stating that the debate about mass surveillance transcends national borders.

The revelations of Edward Snowden marked a turning point in the global perception of privacy in the digital age. Following his leaks, the conversation about the limits of government spying, citizens' rights, and online privacy took on a new dimension, leading to partial reforms in surveillance policies in several countries. In the United States, part of the Patriot Act was reformed through the USA Freedom Act in 2015, although critics argue that it did not go far enough to limit the powers of the NSA.

Snowden is considered by many to be a hero who risked his life to expose abuses of power, while for the US government and some critics, he is seen as a traitor who put national security at risk. The polarization around him reflects the tensions between security and freedom in the digital age.

3. Viktor Kravchenko: The Soviet defector who exposed the horrors of Stalinism

Viktor Andreevich Kravchenko, born on October 11, 1905, in Ekaterinoslav (now Dnipro, Ukraine), was a Soviet defector whose testimony shocked the world during the years following World War II. An industrial engineer and loyal member of the Communist Party of the Soviet Union, Kravchenko left the USSR in 1944, when he was a senior Soviet official on a mission to the United States. His defection, however, was not simply a flight for political or personal reasons, but an open and courageous denunciation of the atrocities of the Stalinist regime. His book "I Chose Freedom" revealed to the world the horrors of collectivization, gulags, and Soviet repression.

Kravchenko grew up in a Ukrainian working-class family, deeply influenced by the revolutionary ideas brewing in the Russian Empire in the early 20th century. At the age of 18, he joined the Communist Party, believing in the promise of an egalitarian society under socialism. Trained as an engineer, he worked on various industrial development projects in the USSR, including the construction of factories and power plants, which led to important positions within the Soviet state apparatus.

During the 1930s, Kravchenko witnessed Stalin's forced collectivization policies, which led to the expropriation of land from peasants and caused mass starvation, especially in Ukraine. It was during this time that he began to question the nature of the regime he had so fervently supported. Hunger, violent repression, and widespread misery marked him deeply, although he continued to maintain his outward loyalty to the Party for fear of being purged.

The breaking point for Kravchenko came during the time of Stalin's Great Purges when thousands of Communist Party members, military officers, and ordinary citizens were arrested, executed, or sent to labor camps in Siberia, known as gulags. Many of his colleagues and close friends were arrested on false charges of treason, and Kravchenko began to feel that the government to which he had dedicated his life was destroying its people.

Despite these feelings, Kravchenko continued to work for the Soviet government, and in 1943 he was sent to the United States as part of an industrial procurement mission to support the Soviet war effort during World War II. He was one of many sent to coordinate the receipt of military supplies under the Lend-Lease Act. However, once in the United States, Kravchenko seized the opportunity to escape, and in 1944, he decided to defect.

Kravchenko carried out his defection in a careful and calculated manner. While working in Washington, D.C., Kravchenko contacted American officials, informing them of his decision to leave the Soviet regime and seek asylum. He knew that by doing so, he would become an enemy of the Soviet state, which would surely seek revenge on him and his family in the USSR.

The American government protected him from immediate retaliation, and Kravchenko took advantage of his newfound freedom to write about the hidden truths of the Soviet regime. In 1946, he published I Chose Freedom, a personal testimony detailing his life in the USSR, the atrocities he witnessed, and the reasons he defected.

Kravchenko's motives for defect were deeply moral and personal. In I Chose Freedom, he explains how he came to realize the contradiction between the promises of socialism and the reality of Stalin's brutal policies. As he progressed in his career within the Soviet state, he witnessed firsthand the suffering of millions of people due to famine, political repression, and concentration camps. Although he had initially believed in the justice of communism, the brutality of the regime led him into a moral dilemma that was impossible to ignore.

Kravchenko concluded that he could no longer be part of a system that inflicted so much suffering on its people. His defection was, in his own words, an act of conscience, a refusal to collaborate with a regime that he believed had betrayed the original ideals of the Bolshevik Revolution.

Kravchenko's book was an immediate success, both in the United States and Europe, and played an important role in revealing to the Western world the realities of the Soviet regime, which until then had been largely unknown or downplayed. It detailed, among other things, the horrors of the gulags, the abuses of the secret police, the NKVD, and the political purges that exterminated thousands of Soviet citizens.

However, the publication of "I Chose Freedom" also made him a target of the Soviet government and its allies in the West. Kravchenko was accused of being an impostor and a liar by the pro-communist press and by several intellectuals who defended the Soviet regime. In 1949, a famous libel trial took place in Paris, known as the "Kravchenko Trial," in which he sued a French communist magazine, Les Lettres Françaises, which had accused Kravchenko of having fabricated his story. The trial became an international scandal, attracting attention around the world.

Kravchenko won the trial, which was seen as a victory for free speech advocates and critics of the Soviet regime. Through his courageous testimony and willingness to stand up to his critics, he cemented his reputation as a whistleblower of Soviet tyranny.

Kravchenko lived out the rest of his life in the United States, writing and speaking about the nature of the Soviet regime. He published a follow-up to his first book in 1950, entitled I Chose Justice, which elaborated on his criticism of human rights abuses in the USSR and his subsequent experience as a defector.

Kravchenko's life was not easy, however. Despite his fame and role as a whistleblower, he lived much of his life in relative isolation, facing personal and financial hardship. He often felt betrayed by the West, seeing that many of the evils he had denounced did not receive the international condemnation he had hoped for. On February 25, 1966, Kravchenko was found dead in his New York apartment. Although his death was ruled a suicide, some theorists have suggested that he may have been murdered by Soviet agents, although there is no conclusive evidence.

Victor Kravchenko was one of the first high-profile defectors to openly denounce the brutalities of Stalin's regime. At a time when many in the West still believed in communism as a viable alternative, her testimony was a warning of the horrors behind the Iron Curtain.

Her courage in making known the realities of Stalinism helped shape public perception of the Soviet regime and played an important role in debates about communism in the Cold War. "I chose freedom" remains a crucial document in the history of Soviet defectors and a fundamental work in the fight for human rights.

4. Boris Karpichkov: The KGB defector who exposed Russia's secrets in the UK

Boris Karpichkov, born in Latvia in 1959, is a former officer of the KGB, the feared Soviet intelligence agency, who defected from Russia and took refuge in the UK. His story is an intricate web of espionage, betrayal, and persecution that illustrates the dangers and risks faced by defectors from the Russian secret services. After years of serving the KGB and its successor, the FSB (Federal Security Service),

Karpichkov fled the system he once served, providing sensitive information to Western intelligence agencies, and making him a target of the Kremlin.

Karpichkov was born in the Latvian Soviet Socialist Republic (then part of the USSR). In the years of the Cold War, he was recruited by the KGB, the powerful intelligence and security agency of the Soviet Union. He was trained as a spy and counterspy, specializing in covert intelligence operations and disinformation.

With the dissolution of the Soviet Union in 1991, Latvia became independent and the KGB structures in the Baltic countries were disbanded. However, many KGB officers, including Karpichkov, went on to work for the Russian intelligence agencies that emerged after the fall of the Soviet regime, such as the FSB, which became the main successor to the KGB.

Despite having worked for years as a loyal member of the Russian secret services, Boris Karpichkov began to question the corrupt and violent system he found himself in. During his years in the FSB, he witnessed how espionage and counterespionage operations became increasingly mixed with corruption, organized crime, and abuse of power. Karpichkov claimed that the FSB had gone from being a national security agency to being an arm of the Russian political and criminal elites.

His discontent grew as he became embroiled in shady operations that threatened not only his safety but also his moral integrity. According to him, he was forced to carry out illegal activities for high-ranking agents who had connections to organized crime. This experience caused him a deep crisis of conscience and led him to become disillusioned with the system he had once defended.

Furthermore, Karpichkov feared for his life, as within the Russian intelligence community there were constant purges and assassinations of those who were seen as a threat or who knew too much. Realizing that his life was in danger, he decided to defect and flee Russia.

In 1998, Boris Karpichkov fled Russia and took refuge in the United Kingdom. Defection was not easy; it involved carefully planning his exit to avoid detection and, most importantly, to be able to offer something in return for the protection of the British authorities. He carried with him a vast amount of confidential information about Russian intelligence operations, which was of great value to MI6, the British intelligence service.

Karpichkov was interrogated for weeks by British intelligence officers, to whom he provided details about Russian spy operations in Europe, including the methods used by the FSB to infiltrate Western countries. This information was key to dismantling Russian spy networks and protecting potential targets in the UK.

Once in the UK, Karpichkov lived under constant threat of reprisals from the Russian government, which considered him a traitor. By his testimony, he has been the target of several assassination attempts, like those suffered by other Russian defectors such as Alexander Litvinenko and Sergei Skripal. He claims to have survived poisonings and attacks by Russian agents who have tried to silence him.

Karpichkov lived for years under false identities provided by the British government to protect his life. Despite this, he has stated in multiple interviews that he fears for his safety and that of his family, as defectors from the Russian security system are considered enemies of the state, and the Kremlin has shown its willingness to pursue and eliminate those it considers traitors.

In 2018, following the attempted assassination of Sergei Skripal and his daughter in Salisbury, Karpichkov made a series of revelations to the media, claiming that he had been warned by contacts in Russia that he was on a blacklist of defectors and oppositionists that the Kremlin planned to eliminate. According to his words, he feared that his life was in danger, as FSB agents and Kremlin-associated groups were actively seeking revenge against him and other defectors.

Karpichkov has claimed on multiple occasions that Russia has used toxic substances and chemical weapons in its attempts to assassinate defectors and oppositionists, something that was corroborated in the case of Litvinenko, who was poisoned with polonium-210 in London, and in the case of Skripal, who was poisoned with the nerve agent Novichok.

Although Karpichkov lives under the protection of the British government, his life has been marked by isolation and constant fear of being assassinated. Unlike other defectors, he has appeared in media outlets and given interviews, in which he has denounced corruption and abuses within the Russian system. This, however, has made him an even clearer target for the Kremlin.

One of the most interesting aspects of Karpichkov's life is how he has managed to survive several assassination attempts, something he has attributed to his KGB training, which taught him to spot threats and avoid dangerous situations. According to him, his knowledge of FSB operations has helped him stay one step ahead of his pursuers.

Boris Karpichkov's story is one of many that exemplify the danger inherent in defection from the Russian intelligence services. His testimony has been instrumental in giving Western agencies a better understanding of the Kremlin's methods in its espionage and retaliation operations. Although he continues to live under threat, Karpichkov has shown extraordinary resilience in surviving in a world where traitors are rarely forgiven.

5. Anatoliy Golitsyn: The defector who shook up Soviet espionage

Anatoliy Golitsyn was a senior KGB officer who defected to the United States in 1961, bringing with him vast knowledge of Soviet intelligence operations. His defection sent shockwaves through the espionage world, as he not only provided key information on KGB activities in the West but also raised controversial theories about communist infiltration on a global level. His life as a defector was marked by controversy, paranoia, and his impact on Western intelligence agencies.

Anatoliy Mikhaylovich Golitsyn was born on August 25, 1926, in Ukraine, then part of the Soviet Union. From a young age, he showed an interest in political and military science, which led him to enter the Soviet military academy and then the KGB, the Soviet Union's main intelligence and security agency. Thanks to his talent and loyalty, he quickly rose through the KGB hierarchy, becoming an expert in covert operations and counterintelligence.

By the late 1950s, Golitsyn was working in the KGB's First Main Directorate, responsible for foreign espionage operations, and was assigned to the Soviet embassy in Helsinki, Finland. From that position, he had access to high-level information about Soviet espionage activities in Western Europe.

In the years leading up to his defection, Anatoliy Golitsyn became increasingly disillusioned with the Soviet regime. He is documented to have deep doubts about communist ideology and the practices of the Soviet government, which he viewed as increasingly corrupt and oppressive. He also had a strong fear that the communist system was not only brutally controlling its citizens, but was covertly expanding its influence around the world, infiltrating governments, organizations, and societies in the West.

Golitsyn realized that there was no way to reform the system from within and began to fear for his safety, especially following internal purges in the KGB. Agents who expressed dissent or showed any sign of doubt about loyalty to the Communist Party were eliminated or imprisoned. This climate of increasing paranoia and repression pushed him to decide to defect.

In 1961, while stationed in Helsinki, Golitsyn took advantage of his position at the Soviet embassy to defect. He contacted the CIA through intermediaries in Finland, offering to defect in exchange for political asylum and protection. The CIA, seeing an opportunity to gain a valuable source of information on KGB activities, quickly arranged for his exfiltration.

Golitsyn was safely brought to the United States, where he began to be intensively interrogated by the CIA and FBI. In his first few weeks of defection, Golitsyn provided a wealth of information about Soviet espionage operations in Europe and elsewhere. He identified numerous undercover Soviet agents operating in the West, allowing American and European intelligence agencies to dismantle several Soviet spy networks.

Although Golitsyn's information was initially invaluable in countering KGB operations, what made him a truly controversial figure was his set of conspiracy theories about a vast global disinformation and deception operation by the Soviet Union. Golitsyn maintained that the Soviets had carried out a "master plan" to infiltrate Western governments and intelligence services, and even suggested that many later defectors were double agents sent to sow distrust in Western intelligence services.

One of his most controversial claims was that Eastern European leaders who were critical of the Soviet Union, such as Yugoslavia under Tito or the breakup of China and the USSR under Mao Zedong, were part of an elaborate Soviet plan to deceive the West. According to Golitsyn, it was all a facade to convince the world that communism was fragmented, when in fact it remained a unified force with a common goal: global domination.

One of Golitsyn's most shocking revelations was his claim that Kim Philby, one of the most senior officers in British intelligence, had been a Soviet spy. This turned out to be true, and the exposure of Philby, along with other members of the Cambridge Circle, shook the foundations of MI6 and the British intelligence service.

While the information Golitsyn provided about Soviet spies was confirmed in many cases, his theories about the great global communist conspiracy were met with skepticism. Within the CIA, these theories created divisions. One section of the agency, led by counterintelligence chief James Jesus Angleton, believed Golitsyn's claims and adopted a stance of extreme caution, seeing potential traitors and undercover Soviet agents at all levels of the U.S. government.

On the other hand, many officers in the CIA and other intelligence agencies felt that Golitsyn was exaggerating and that his conspiracy theories were not sufficiently substantiated. Tensions grew to the point that some later defectors, such as Yuri Nosenko, were treated with extreme suspicion and considered double agents by those who supported Golitsyn's ideas.

After his defection, Golitsyn was relocated to a secret location in the United States, where he lived under protection. He published a book entitled "New Lies for Old" in 1984, in which he set out his theories about Soviet deception and the master plan to misinform the West. In this book, Golitsyn predicted the eventual fall of the Soviet Union but argued that this fall would be a tactic to fool the West and get communist countries to infiltrate even deeper into liberal democracies.

Over the years, Golitsyn kept a low profile and avoided the media, which only added to the mystique around him. Although some considered him a hero who had exposed the corruption and lies of the KGB, others saw him as a paranoid whose theories had caused more harm than good.

Anatoliy Golitsyn died in 2008, leaving a mixed legacy in the history of espionage. For some, he was one of the most important defectors of the Cold War, whose warnings about Soviet infiltration helped protect the West. For others, he was a man who gripped by paranoia, sowed distrust within the very ranks of the Western intelligence services.

Despite the controversy that surrounded him, it is undeniable that Golitsyn had a lasting impact on the Western intelligence community. His defection marked one of the most important moments in the struggle between power blocs during the Cold War and continues to be studied by historians and espionage experts as one of the most intriguing and enigmatic cases of the era.

6. No Kum-sok (Kenneth Rowe): The North Korean defector who defied the communist regime

No Kum-sok, later known as Kenneth Rowe, is one of North Korea's most iconic defectors, famous for his daring escape in 1953 when he flew a MiG-15 fighter jet into South Korea. His defection carried out amid the tense atmosphere of the Korean War, not only represented a propaganda victory for the West but also brought with him a crucial piece of Soviet military technology. His story is a tale of bravery, frustration in the face of an oppressive regime, and the quest for freedom.

No Kum-sok was born on January 10, 1932, in the region that, after World War II, would become North Korea. In his early years, Korea was under Japanese occupation, and No's life was spent in a country marked by oppression and foreign occupation. When Japan was defeated in 1945, Korea was divided into two: the northern part came under Soviet influence, while the south was supported by the United States. This division created fertile ground for the rise of a communist regime under the leadership of Kim Il-sung, which began the creation of the North Korea we know today.

No Kum was raised in an environment of strict communist ideology, where total devotion to the state and Kim Il-sung was taught. As a talented young man, he was recruited into the North Korean army and later became a fighter pilot. During the Korean War (1950-1953), No Kum flew a MiG-15 fighter, an advanced fighter plane supplied by the Soviet Union to North Korea.

Despite intense communist propaganda and tight state control in North Korea, No Kum-sok had become a skeptic of the regime. In his own words, he was never a true believer in communist ideology. From a young age, he dreamed of a life outside the oppression of North Korea, and his disillusionment only grew with time. Poverty, constant fear of political reprisals, and lack of personal freedom led him to plan his escape.

No Kum admired the freedoms that the United States and the West represented. Despite the intense surveillance under which North Koreans lived, he had absorbed information about the outside world through clandestine means and was convinced that his future did not lie in North Korea. Added to this was his discontent with the brutality of Kim Il-sung's regime, which demanded blind loyalty and severely punished any dissent.

On September 21, 1953, No Kum-sok, at just 21 years old, made one of the bravest and riskiest decisions of his life. Despite enormous personal risk and the odds stacked against him, he flew his MiG-15 fighter from an air base in North Korea to Kimpo Air Base in South Korea, just 15 minutes away. What is remarkable about his escape is that he did so without informing anyone of his intentions. In the early morning, he took off as if it were a routine training mission and headed south.

The MiG-15 was one of the most advanced aircraft of the time, and its technology was of great interest to the United States and its allies, as it had been used by communist forces in the Korean War with great effectiveness against Western aircraft.

Incredibly, No Kum flew undetected by South Korean and American air defenses, as radars did not pick up his plane until it landed at Kimpo Air Base. His defection was so sudden that the soldiers at the South Korean base, seeing him arrive, thought it was an enemy aircraft on a mission, so there was initially confusion and alarm. However, when No Kum emerged from the cockpit of the MiG-15, raising his arms in surrender, it became clear that he was a defector.

After landing, No Kum-sok was greeted with disbelief, but also with satisfaction. American intelligence interrogated him extensively to obtain information about both North Korean military operations and the characteristics of the MiG-15. The capture of this fighter was a blow to the communists and a valuable bonus for the Americans, who had the opportunity to closely analyze the advanced technology of the Soviet aircraft.

At the time, the US government had offered a $100,000 reward to any North Korean or Chinese pilot who would defect and hand over a MiG-15. Although No Kum-sok was unaware of the reward, he received the money and was resettled in the United States, where he eventually adopted the name Kenneth Rowe.

After his defection, No Kum-sok moved to the United States, where he began a new life. At first, he was taken to several locations to ensure his safety, as authorities feared reprisals from North Korean or Soviet communist agents. Once his situation stabilized, No

Kum studied engineering at the University of Delaware, which allowed him to forge a successful career in the aerospace industry. He worked for major American companies, including Grumman Aerospace and General Motors, participating in various technological projects.

Adopting the name Kenneth Rowe was part of his integration into American life, and in the years that followed, he became a U.S. citizen. Yet, despite his success in his new homeland, the shadow of North Korea was ever-present in his life.

No Kum-sok became a symbol of the fight for freedom against communist oppression. His defection represented not only a tactical victory for the United States in the Cold War but also a potent act of defiance against one of the most oppressive regimes in the world.

In 1996, No Kum published his autobiography, "My Road to Freedom: The MiG-15 and Me," in which he recounted his extraordinary life, from his youth in North Korea to his escape to South Korea and his later life in the United States. In his book, he reflected on the motivations behind his defection and how freedom, both personal and political, had been his greatest drive.

Kenneth Rowe, as he became known in his new life, lived as an American citizen until his passing in 2022. His story remains one of the most notable in the context of military defections during the Cold War, and his daring flight in a MiG-15 is still remembered as an example of resistance to tyranny.

Even though his defection was greeted with enthusiasm by the West, the life of a defector is never easy. No Kum-sok, although he was financially rewarded and given asylum in the United States, lived for a long time under the shadow of the regime. North Korean. Defecting from a country as hermetic as North Korea meant giving up any chance of returning to his homeland or seeing his family again.

In his autobiography, No Kum-sok (Kenneth Rowe) reflected on the emotional and psychological hardships he faced as a defector. "Although I found freedom and opportunity in America, the personal cost was significant," he wrote. Like many defectors, he faced the challenge of adjusting to a new culture, learning a new language, and rebuilding his life from scratch.

Today, No Kum-sok's defection is seen not only as an important event in the Korean War but as a milestone in the fight against communist dictatorship. North Korea remains one of the most repressive countries in the world, and No Kum-sok's escape in 1953 represents an act of bravery that has inspired many other defectors since.

In his later years, Kenneth Rowe lived a quiet life in the United States, where he continued to work as an aerospace engineer. Although he avoided active involvement in politics or controversy, he occasionally shared his story in lectures and interviews, recounting his incredible abandonment and reflecting on life under a totalitarian regime.

Rowe passed away on December 26, 2022, at age 90, leaving behind a legacy as one of the most celebrated defectors of the Cold War. His life, marked by courage and a desire for freedom, remains a powerful testament to human resilience in the face of oppression and injustice.

7. Mikhail Baryshnikov: The dancer who dazzled the world with his artistry and his abandonment

Mikhail Baryshnikov is one of the most celebrated dancers of all time, known for his virtuosity, his charisma, and his ability to take ballet to new heights in both the Soviet Union and the West. However, his fame is not only due to his impressive artistic career but also to his bold decision to defect from the Soviet Union in 1974 to seek artistic freedom in the Western world. His defection marked a key moment in the history of dance, and his later life became a showcase for the power of art to transcend political and cultural boundaries.

Mikhail Nikolayevich Baryshnikov was born on January 27, 1948, in Riga, Latvia, then part of the Soviet Union. His childhood was marked by the strict rules of the Soviet regime, but also by the cultural richness that ballet offered in the country. From an early age, Baryshnikov displayed an exceptional talent for dance. At age 12, he began training at the Kirov Theatre Ballet School in Leningrad (now St. Petersburg), one of the most prestigious dance academies in the world.

In 1967, he made his debut at the Kirov Theatre (now the Mariinsky Theatre), where he quickly stood out for his impeccable technique and electrifying stage presence. Despite the rigidity of the Soviet-style, Baryshnikov showed an interest in expanding his repertoire, which would soon lead him to question the limitations imposed by the Soviet system.

As his fame in the Soviet Union grew, so did his frustration with the restrictions the communist regime placed on artists. Cultural censorship, limited opportunities to work with Western choreographers, and strict government control over the personal and professional lives of dancers influenced Baryshnikov's decision to seek a freer life in the West.

Art and dance were seen in the Soviet Union as a tool of state propaganda. This meant that talented artists like Baryshnikov were used to project the cultural supremacy of Communism but at the cost of their creative freedom. Baryshnikov felt increasingly constrained by the obligation to follow a ballet tradition that, while technical and rigorous, did not allow him to explore new forms of artistic expression, especially in contemporary dance.

In addition, during his international tours, Baryshnikov began to interact with other dancers and choreographers from the Western world, which broadened his vision of what ballet could become. Inspired by figures like George Balanchine and Jerome Robbins, who were revolutionizing ballet in the West, Baryshnikov became convinced that he could only reach his full artistic potential outside the Soviet Union.

Mikhail Baryshnikov's defection took place on June 29, 1974, in the middle of a tour of the Kirov Theatre in Canada. The dancer took advantage of a performance in Toronto to put his escape plan into action. During the tour, Baryshnikov had been in contact with friends and supporters in the West who helped him coordinate his defection.

On the day of his defection, after a performance in Toronto, Baryshnikov simply left the hotel where the ballet troupe was staying and met with Canadian agents who provided him with protection. This action was a blow to the Soviet regime, which immediately declared him a traitor and erased his name from the official history of ballet in the USSR.

Baryshnikov sought asylum in Canada and soon after moved to the United States, where he was enthusiastically welcomed by the ballet world. His departure was not only a highly symbolic event in the context of the Cold War but also marked the beginning of a new era in his artistic career.

Once in the West, Baryshnikov was welcomed with open arms by leading ballet and contemporary dance companies. In 1974, shortly after his departure, he joined the American Ballet Theatre (ABT), where he quickly became one of the brightest stars. During this period, the dancer not only performed classical roles but also began working with contemporary choreographers, which allowed him to explore new dance forms and expand his repertoire.

In 1978, Baryshnikov was appointed artistic director of the American Ballet Theatre, a position he held until 1980. During his tenure, he promoted the creation of new ballet works, inviting contemporary choreographers to collaborate with the company, which cemented his reputation as an innovator. in the world of dance.

One of the highlights of his career in the West was his participation in the film "The Turning Point" (1977), for which he received an Oscar nomination for Best Supporting Actor. In addition, his role in the film "White Nights" (1985), alongside fellow Russian defector dancer Rudolf Nureyev, was a cinematic reflection of his own experiences as an exiled dancer.

In 1990, Baryshnikov founded his own company, the White Oak Dance Project, together with choreographer Mark Morris, to promote contemporary dance. This decision marked an important turn in his career, as he dedicated himself to exploring new forms of dance and working with innovative choreographers.

Mikhail Baryshnikov became an American citizen and has lived much of his life in New York. His career spanned several decades, and although he retired from classical dance, he continued to be actively involved in contemporary dance and acting projects. His legacy is unquestionable: he is considered one of the greatest dancers of the 20th century, and his influence on ballet and contemporary dance is profound.

In addition to his artistic career, Baryshnikov has been an advocate for human rights and artistic freedom.

Throughout his life, he has spoken openly about the difficulties of living under a totalitarian regime and has supported other artists exiled from repressive regimes.

In 2005, Baryshnikov opened the Baryshnikov Arts Center in New York, a space dedicated to innovation in dance, theater, and music. This center is an extension of his vision to support new generations of artists and give them a space to experiment and develop their art.

Mikhail Baryshnikov's defection was not only a political decision or a flight from an oppressive regime, but also a search for artistic freedom. His talent, passion, and desire to innovate led him to escape the restrictions imposed by the Soviet Union, and his career in the West became one of the most influential in the history of ballet. His life and work remain a testament to the power of art to transcend borders and limitations, and his legacy continues to inspire dancers and artists around the world.

8. Oleg Gordievsky: The defector who revealed KGB secrets to the UK

Oleg Gordievsky is one of the most significant figures of the Cold War, best known for being a senior KGB officer (the Soviet intelligence service) who defected to the UK. His defection in 1985 was a devastating blow to Soviet intelligence and a major triumph for Western secret services. Throughout his career as a double agent, Gordievsky provided key information on KGB operations and played a crucial role in the relationship between the West and the Soviet Union during the final years of the Cold War.

Oleg Antonovich Gordievsky was born on 10 October 1938 in Moscow, to a family with deep roots in Soviet intelligence. His father worked for the NKVD, the predecessor of the KGB, and his older brother also joined Soviet intelligence. From an early age, Oleg was destined to follow in his family's footsteps.

He joined the KGB in 1962 and was assigned to the International Relations Department. After completing his training, Gordievsky was sent to work in several Soviet embassies abroad, including an assignment in Denmark in 1966. During his time in Denmark, he was responsible for monitoring foreign diplomats and carrying out espionage activities. His rise within the KGB was rapid, due to his dedication and competence.

Despite his initial loyalty to the KGB, Gordievsky began to develop strong doubts about the Soviet regime, particularly after the events of the Prague Spring in 1968, when Warsaw Pact troops invaded Czechoslovakia to suppress democratizing reforms. These events made him see the true authoritarian and oppressive face of Soviet Communism, which showed in him a growing disenchantment with the system.

In addition to internal political repression, Gordievsky was dissatisfied with the corruption and double standards prevalent among Soviet leaders. He believed that the USSR did not represent the values of justice and fairness that were proclaimed but was instead an authoritarian regime that exercised control through intimidation and repression. This disillusionment led him to question his loyalty and eventually to consider betraying his country.

Gordievsky's contact with British intelligence, MI6, began in 1974, during his second stint in Denmark. The British, who already had him on their radar as a potential source of information, approached him, taking advantage of his growing disenchantment with the Soviet regime. Gordievsky was hesitant at first, but eventually decided to collaborate with the British, motivated by his desire to fight what he saw as the injustice and oppression of Soviet communism.

Gordievsky began working as a double agent, providing MI6 with a significant amount of information about the KGB's operations and strategies in the West. His relationship with the British was extremely fruitful: in the following years, he supplied key details about the KGB's structure, its espionage methods, and its efforts to influence the politics of Western countries.

In 1982, Gordievsky was transferred to London, where he was appointed as head of the KGB station in the United Kingdom, a highly prominent position. This position allowed him access to even more sensitive information, and his reports to the British played a crucial role in the West's understanding of Soviet operations.

Among the information he provided, his role in alerting the West to Soviet fears of a preemptive nuclear strike by NATO in the 1980s stands out. Such was the paranoia of Soviet leaders regarding a Western attack that the USSR was willing to take preemptive action, and Gordievsky informed the British and Americans of this mindset, helping to calm tensions and prevent a major conflict.

However, despite his years of loyal service in MI6, the KGB began to suspect Gordievsky. In May 1985, he was summoned back to Moscow for "consultations" - a pretext used by the Soviets to interrogate those who were under suspicion of treason. Although Gordievsky was aware of the danger, he had no choice but to return.

In Moscow, he was subjected to intense interrogation and mind-altering drug poisoning techniques designed to extract confessions without resorting to physical violence. Although Gordievsky never confessed, it was clear that his position was extremely dangerous, and MI6 activated an escape plan to get him out of the Soviet Union.

Gordievsky's escape plan, known as "Operation Pimlico," was one of the most daring and successful carried out by MI6 during the Cold War. In this escape, one of the most dramatic of the Cold War, Gordievsky managed to evade Soviet surveillance and made his way to a prearranged rendezvous point near the Finnish border, where MI6 agents recognized him and smuggled him out of the USSR. The operation was extremely risky but successful. Gordievsky was flown first to Finland and then to the United Kingdom, where he was welcomed as a hero by British intelligence.

After his defection, Gordievsky developed in the United Kingdom, where he has lived ever since under British protection. Although his defection was a major blow to the KGB, the Soviet authorities never managed to capture him. In retaliation, he was sentenced to death in absentia for treason, and to this day lives with the threat of Russian reprisals.

Gordievsky was one of the key informants who helped the West understand the paranoia of Soviet leaders during the 1983 Exercise Able Archer crisis, a NATO drill that the USSR interpreted as preparation for a nuclear attack.

In 2007, Gordievsky was awarded the Order of St Michael and St George, an honor bestowed by Queen Elizabeth II for his "exceptional service to the security of the United Kingdom."

Over the years, Gordievsky has written several books about his life in the KGB and his experiences as a double agent, including "Next Stop Execution" and "KGB: The Inside Story," where he details the internal operations and structures of Soviet intelligence. His revelations have been instrumental in understanding the workings of the KGB during the tensest years of the Cold War.

Despite living under constant surveillance and with a semi-secret identity, Gordievsky has maintained a relatively high profile in the media and has continued to share his experience with the public. His contribution to British and Western intelligence is immeasurable, and he has been recognized as one of the most valuable agents ever to have worked for MI6.

9. Nadia Comăneci: From Olympic star to defector in search of freedom

Nadia Comăneci is one of the most celebrated and admired athletes in the history of sport. Born in Romania during the time of Nicolae Ceaușescu's communist dictatorship, Nadia stood out from a young age as an exceptional gymnast, achieving worldwide fame after her historic performance at the Montreal Olympics in 1976, where she became the first gymnast to earn a perfect score of 10. Despite her achievements, her personal and professional life was marked by the restrictions and pressures of the Romanian communist regime. In 1989, seeking to escape the oppression of her country, Nadia defected from Romania and started a new life in the United States.

Nadia Comăneci was born on November 12, 1961, in Gheorgheni, Romania, and grew up in the small town of Onești. At an early age, she began training in gymnastics under coaches Béla and Márta Károlyi, who spotted her extraordinary potential. By the age of 13, Nadia was already competing on the international stage, scoring major victories at the 1975 European Championships.

Her global breakthrough came at the Montreal Olympics in 1976, where, at the age of 14, Nadia stunned the world by earning the first perfect score in Olympic gymnastics history – a feat she would repeat six more times during the same Games. She won three gold medals, one silver, and one bronze, becoming a global sporting icon and a source of national pride for the Ceaușescu communist government, which exploited her success for propaganda purposes.

Despite her international celebrity status, Nadia's life in Romania was not easy. Nicolae Ceaușescu's communist regime controlled every aspect of her life. She became a propaganda tool, used to project a positive image of Romania abroad. Her private life was under constant surveillance, and although she was acclaimed for her achievements, the pressure she was under as a representative of a country under a totalitarian regime was immense.

Following the Moscow Olympics in 1980, where she won further medals, including a gold, Nadia began to experience a decline in her performance and suffered injuries. At the same time, tensions within her personal life also increased. Coaches Béla and Márta Károlyi defected to the United States in 1981, weakening her support team. In addition, Nadia began to feel the weight of social isolation, lack of freedom, and oppressive conditions suffered by the Romanian people under Ceaușescu's iron grip.

In the 1980s, the situation in Romania under the dictator's regime deteriorated further and further. Living conditions worsened due to the president's disastrous economic policies, and repression intensified. Although Nadia remained a public figure, her personal life was restricted, and she felt she had no control over her destiny. Professional and personal opportunities in Romania were limited by the lack of freedom.

Amidst this growing despair, Nadia made the brave decision to defect in search of freedom and better opportunities. In addition to political oppression, personal pressures and controls imposed on her life also influenced her decision.

On November 27, 1989, just weeks before the fall of the Ceaușescu regime, Nadia Comăneci set out on a dangerous journey to freedom. With the help of a group of friends who knew the clandestine escape routes, Nadia illegally crossed the border into Hungary. From there, she continued to Austria and eventually sought asylum in the United States.

Nadia's defection was extremely risky, as Romania's borders were heavily guarded, and defectors faced the possibility of arrest or murder if caught. Upon her arrival in the United States, Nadia was greeted with great media interest, but she kept a relatively low profile for the first few months as she adjusted to her new life.

Once in the United States, Nadia began a new phase in her life. In 1994, she met former American gymnast Bart Conner, whom she married in 1996. Together, they opened a gymnastics school and worked to promote the sport. Nadia became an American citizen and has lived in the United States ever since.

Comăneci has continued to be an influential figure in the world of sport and an ambassador for gymnastics. Over the years, she has been involved in various charities and has promoted health and well-being, particularly in her native Romania, to which she has returned on several occasions after the fall of the communist regime.

Nadia has received numerous awards and honors throughout her life and is considered one of the greatest gymnasts of all time.

10. Ion Mihai Pacepa: The Highest-Ranking Defector from the Communist Bloc

Ion Mihai Pacepa (1928-2021) was a high-ranking officer in the intelligence service of Communist Romania and the highest-ranking defector from any Warsaw Pact country. His defection to the United States in 1978 shook the foundations of the Romanian regime and sent shockwaves through the international intelligence community. Pacepa not only revealed internal secrets of Nicolae Ceauşescu's government but also provided valuable information about the espionage operations of the KGB and other Soviet bloc intelligence services.

Born on October 28, 1928, in Bucharest, Romania, Pacepa joined the Securitate, the Romanian state intelligence and security service, in the 1950s, after completing studies in chemical engineering and briefly working in the oil industry. Throughout his career in the Securitate, he rose through the ranks to occupy senior positions within the communist regime's security apparatus. During the 1970s, he became Ceauşescu's advisor, as well as head of foreign intelligence (DIE) and secretary of state.

Romanian intelligence had deep ties to the KGB and other Soviet bloc agencies. Pacepa oversaw espionage activities directed not only against the West but also against other communist bloc countries, due to Ceaușescu's ambitions to exert greater influence within the Warsaw Pact. The Romanian leader maintained a façade of independence from Moscow, but carried out brutal internal repression, supported by the Securitate.

Ion Mihai Pacepa defected for multiple reasons, both ideological and personal. Throughout his years in the Securitate, he began to become disenchanted with the practices of the Ceaușescu regime, especially the rampant corruption and the dictator's cult of personality. Ceaușescu had established a totalitarian regime, in which both the party and the government operated under brutal repression, and the lives of Romanians deteriorated restrictively.

Pacepa was also dismayed by the illegal activities he was involved in as an intelligence officer. One of the turning points was his involvement in covert operations aimed at destroying the reputation of Western figures through disinformation and defamation campaigns. The regime also engaged in acts of industrial and political espionage, as well as arms trafficking, which went against the beliefs Pacepa had held in his early years.

He also feared for his life. In the Securitate, even high-ranking officers were not safe from purges or punishment if Ceaușescu began to suspect their loyalty. This fear, coupled with growing dissatisfaction with the regime, prompted him to make the dangerous decision to defect.

In July 1978, Ion Mihai Pacepa was called to Bonn, West Germany, to participate in a meeting with representatives of the East German government. It was during this trip that he contacted the CIA to defect. The decision was not an easy one; it meant abandoning his life in Romania, risking retaliation against his family, and becoming a target of the regime. However, the CIA quickly agreed to help him.

The defection operation was carried out in secret. Pacepa was filtered from West Germany to the United States, where he was granted political asylum and a new identity. Once on American soil, he began to collaborate closely with the CIA, providing crucial information on Romanian intelligence operations as well as the broader activities of the communist bloc.

His defection was a devastating blow to Ceaușescu, who launched an international manhunt to find and eliminate Pacepa. Assassination orders were issued, and the Romanian dictator even offered a two-million-dollar bounty on his head. In addition, the regime spread propaganda accusing Pacepa of being a traitor and collaborator of Western imperialism. However, the CIA protected Pacepa with a new identity and kept him out of the reach of the Romanian authorities.

Following his defection, Pacepa wrote several books and articles that exposed the ins and outs of communist espionage and the character of the Ceaușescu regime. His most famous book, Red Horizons: Chronicles of a Communist Spymaster (1987), detailed the massive corruption and abuse of power by Ceaușescu and his wife, Elena. This book was particularly explosive because it revealed how

Ceauşescu and other communist leaders were deeply involved in criminal activities and personal enrichment.

Pacepa's revelations affected not only Romania but also the operations of the KGB and other intelligence services in the Soviet bloc. It exposed methods of disinformation used to influence Western politics, espionage campaigns, and efforts to destabilize governments around the world. Western intelligence agencies widely valued the information Pacepa provided them with.

One of the most startling accusations he made was that the KGB and other communist services were behind many of the conspiracies and manipulations that shocked the West during the Cold War. He noted that the USSR used a vast network of psychological operations and disinformation campaigns to undermine Western governments and sow chaos in their societies.

Over the years, several attempts were made to assassinate Pacepa in the United States. The Securitate hired terrorists such as Ilich Ramirez Sanchez (better known as Carlos the Jackal) to eliminate him, but none of these attempts were successful.

Pacepa lived the rest of his life in the United States, occasionally collaborating with Western media outlets and intelligence agencies. His publications continue to be an important source for understanding the methods of communist espionage and covert operations carried out by Soviet bloc regimes.

Pacepa passed away on February 14, 2021, at the age of 92. Despite the controversy surrounding his defection, he is considered a key figure in exposing the hidden realities of communism and intelligence operations in the Cold War. His bravery in defecting and his contributions to Western intelligence have left a lasting mark on the history of espionage.

11. Orestes Lorenzo: The Cuban Pilot Who Defied the Regime for Freedom

Orestes Lorenzo Pérez, a Cuban Air Force fighter pilot, became world famous for his daring defection and risky operation to rescue his family from the Cuban regime. Born in Cuba, Lorenzo was trained as a military pilot, rising to the rank of major in the Air Force. His life changed radically in 1991, when he decided to escape the island in search of freedom, leaving behind a military career and his family, who would remain under the strict surveillance of the Cuban government.

Throughout his time in the armed forces, Lorenzo became disillusioned with Fidel Castro's communist regime. He witnessed the increasing restrictions on individual freedoms, political repression, poverty, and isolation in Cuba. Like many Cubans, Lorenzo longed for a better future for himself and his family. He not only wanted to flee the oppressive control of the regime but also to offer his children the chance to live in freedom. He decided that he could no longer serve a government in which he did not believe.

On March 20, 1991, Lorenzo took advantage of a routine training flight in his MiG-23 fighter jet, one of the most advanced military aircraft in the possession of the Cuban military. Without warning, Lorenzo changed course and flew into the Straits of Florida, heading for Key West, Florida, where he landed at the Boca Chica Naval Base. His defection was swift and effective, surprising both his superiors in Cuba and the U.S. authorities.

Lorenzo's flight to freedom was extremely risky, as any attempt at defection was severely punished by the Castro regime, and Cuban pilots were closely monitored. In addition, the possibility of being intercepted by U.S. air defense forces also posed a danger. However, Lorenzo achieved his goal without incident, and after his landing, he requested political asylum in the United States.

Despite his initial success, Lorenzo did not consider his mission complete, as his wife, Victoria, and two sons, Reinaldo and Alejandro, remained trapped in Cuba, under the regime's control. The Cuban government repeatedly denied Lorenzo's requests for his family to join him in the United States. Fidel Castro used this tactic to punish defectors, holding their family's hostage on the island.

Frustrated by the lack of diplomatic results and Castro's repressive tactics, Lorenzo decided to take matters into his own hands. He devised a bold plan to rescue his family. In December 1992, he flew a small, unarmed, unregistered Cessna 310 plane from Florida to Cuba. Lorenzo knew that the success of this mission would depend on precision and speed: he could not be detected or intercepted.

On December 19, 1992, Lorenzo landed on a road near El Mamey beach on the northern coast of Cuba, where his wife and children were secretly waiting for him. The landing was quick and precise. In just 90 seconds, his family was on board, and Lorenzo took off before Cuban authorities could react. He flew back to Florida, achieving the rescue in an operation that seemed straight out of an action movie.

The successful rescue operation of Orestes Lorenzo attracted international attention and was seen as a humiliation for the Cuban regime. The story of a man who not only deserted Castro's army but also openly defied the government to rescue his family made him a symbol of resistance against oppression and the fight for freedom.

After the rescue, Lorenzo and his family settled in the United States, where they were received with admiration and support. Lorenzo was hailed as a hero, and his story became an inspiring example for many Cubans who also wished to escape the oppression of the communist regime.

After reuniting with his family in the United States, Lorenzo began a new life. He wrote a book titled "Flight to Freedom," in which he recounted his story, from his defection to the rescue of his family. He became a frequent speaker on human rights and freedom issues, denouncing Cuban government abuses and actively working in the Cuban exile community.

Orestes Lorenzo and his family lived their new life in freedom in the United States, far from the repression of the regime he once served. His defection and the rescue of his family remain one of the most audacious and dramatic stories in the history of Cuban defections.

Orestes Lorenzo is an example of courage and determination in the fight for freedom. His defection was not only an act of personal defiance against Fidel Castro's regime but also a testament of love and dedication to his family. His heroic rescue and bravery made him a legend among Cuban defectors, and his story remains an inspiration to those longing to escape oppression in search of a better future.

12. Viktor Belenko: The pilot who defected to the West with a Soviet fighter jet

Viktor Ivanovich Belenko is one of the most famous defectors of the Cold War due to the spectacular nature of his escape, which included flying an advanced Soviet MiG-25 fighter jet to Japan and then seeking political asylum in the United States. His defection in 1976 was a blow to the Soviet Union and provided the West with critical information about Soviet military technology.

Viktor Belenko was born on February 15, 1947, in Nalchik, in the then-Soviet territory of Kabardino-Balkaria. He grew up in the Soviet Union in an era marked by intense Cold War competition between the two superpowers, the USSR and the United States.

Fascinated by aviation from a young age, Belenko joined the Soviet Air Force and was trained as a fighter pilot.

Eventually, Belenko was assigned to fly the advanced MiG-25 Foxbat, an aircraft that was once considered one of the fastest and most powerful in the world. The MiG-25 was primarily designed as a high-altitude interceptor capable of flying at supersonic speeds and taking on high-tech American spy planes and bombers such as the SR-71 Blackbird.

Despite being a prominent member of the Soviet Air Force, Belenko was deeply dissatisfied with life under communist rule. He became disillusioned with the Soviet system for several reasons: political repression, lack of individual freedoms, and the state's absolute control over all aspects of life. Living conditions, economic deprivation, and propaganda attempting to conceal the realities of Soviet life also contributed to his growing resentment.

Furthermore, Belenko was frustrated with the way pilots and other high-level military personnel were treated. Although they were part of an elite in the professional sense, they suffered many of the same deprivations as the rest of the Soviet population, which further fueled his desire to escape and seek a better life.

On September 6, 1976, Viktor Belenko decided to execute his defection plan. That day, he took off from a Soviet air base in the Eastern Siberia region in his MiG-25, simulating a routine training mission.

However, mid-flight he changed course and flew toward Japan.

The plane traveled at supersonic speeds and, after hours of flight, Belenko landed at Hakodate Airport on the island of Hokkaido, Japan. Due to the surprise of the Japanese authorities, the MiG-25 overshot the runway and stopped in a nearby field. The crash landing slightly damaged the aircraft, but both Belenko and MiG-25 were saved without major incidents.

Belenko immediately requested political asylum, claiming that he could not continue living under communist rule and that he desired freedom in the West. The Japanese authorities, along with the United States government, welcomed him and transported him to safe territory.

Viktor Belenko's defection was a devastating blow to the Soviet Union. Not only had they lost a highly trained pilot, but their prized fighter jet, the MiG-25, was also in the hands of the West. For American intelligence and its allies, the capture of the MiG-25 was a gold mine. For years, NATO had speculated about the capabilities of this aircraft, which was believed to be invincible in combat and technologically advanced. Detailed inspection of the aircraft allowed Western engineers and analysts to discover that although the MiG-25 was extremely fast, it also had significant deficiencies in its design and technology, which diminished the perceived threat of the aircraft.

Japan allowed the plane to be inspected by American specialists before it was returned to the Soviet Union, dismantled into parts, and carefully studied.

After his defection, Belenko was quickly flown to the United States, where he was given political asylum and began a new life. The CIA protected him and used his knowledge to gain insight into Soviet military capabilities as well as Soviet Air Force operations. Belenko also provided valuable information on Soviet training procedures and combat doctrine.

Once in the United States, Belenko adjusted to life in the Western world and wrote a book about his life and escape titled "MiG Pilot: The Final Escape of Lieutenant Belenko," published in 1980. The book was co-written by John Barron and details both his life in the Soviet Union and the circumstances that led to his defection.

Belenko also married in the United States and lived a relatively quiet life away from the spotlight. His defection was a symbol of the discontent that some of the highest members of the Soviet military establishment felt towards the communist system.

Belenko's defection had important political repercussions. The Soviet Union demanded the immediate return of its pilot and his plane, which Japan only partially complied with by returning the dismantled plane. In addition, the Soviets accused the United States of orchestrating the defection, which was denied by the Americans. In Soviet propaganda, Belenko was labeled a traitor and a coward.

In the West, he was seen as a Cold War hero, a figure who risked everything for freedom and who provided invaluable information about Soviet military might.

13. Lee Harvey Oswald: The American defector and his enigmatic passage through the Soviet Union

Lee Harvey Oswald is one of the most notorious defectors in modern history due to his role in one of the most tragic events of the 20th century: the assassination of President John F. Kennedy in 1963. Before this event, Oswald had defected from the United States to the Soviet Union in 1959, which marked a peculiar and controversial phase of his life.

Lee Harvey Oswald was born on October 18, 1939, in New Orleans, Louisiana. He grew up in a family facing economic difficulties, and his childhood was marked by instability. His father died shortly before his birth, and his mother had to raise him alone. From an early age, Oswald showed signs of emotional maladjustment, and throughout his adolescence, he was moved between several cities and schools, which aggravated his sense of alienation.

During his youth, Oswald developed a growing interest in political ideologies, particularly Marxism. Despite growing up in an anti-communist context, such as Cold War America, Oswald embraced communism and was drawn to the Soviet Union, which he viewed as a bastion of social justice and economic equity.

In 1956, at the age of 17, Oswald enlisted in the United States Marine Corps. During his time in the military, he was trained as a radar operator and achieved a minimum qualification with the rifle, later contradicting the idea that he was an expert marksman. It was around this time that Oswald began to openly express his communist sympathies and his growing admiration for the Soviet Union.

In 1959, after receiving an honorable discharge, Oswald made the bold decision to defect. He traveled to Moscow to renounce his American citizenship and become a Soviet citizen. His desire to escape what he saw as the hypocrisy and imperialism of the United States led him to seek a new life under the communist system, which he idealized from a distance.

Oswald arrived in the Soviet Union in October 1959 and declared to the Soviet authorities that he wished to renounce his American citizenship. However, the Soviets did not initially welcome him with open arms. Rather than being regarded as a hero, the Soviet authorities were suspicious of his true intentions and worried that he might be a spy or simply a diplomatic liability.

Despite these initial misgivings, Oswald was allowed to stay in the Soviet Union. He was sent to live in Minsk, in the then-Byelorussian Soviet Socialist Republic, where he was assigned a job in a radio factory. Although the living conditions he was offered were significantly better than those of most Soviets (he was even provided with an apartment), Oswald soon became disillusioned with the communist system he had idolized. He found that life in the Soviet Union was not as ideal as he had imagined; There was censorship, a lack of personal freedoms, and constant state surveillance.

While living in Minsk, Oswald met Marina Prusákova, a young woman whom he married in 1961. Marina became a key figure in Oswald's life, and together they had a daughter, in June 1962. However, despite his new family and the apparent success of having managed to defect, Oswald began to feel the weight of Soviet life, full of restrictions and disillusionment.

To the surprise of many, after having defected from the United States and renounced his citizenship, Oswald requested to return to his native country in 1962. Although he initially faced some resistance from the American authorities, he was eventually allowed to return to the United States, along with his wife Marina and their daughter. This decision provoked suspicions in both the United States and the Soviet Union. Some wondered whether Oswald had been "reconverted" to spy on the Soviets, although no conclusive evidence has been found that Oswald was a spy.

Upon his return, Oswald continued his extreme political stances. He briefly settled in Texas and remained in contact with pro-Castro and pro-communist groups. His life, however, was marked by increasing emotional instability, a precarious financial situation, and a strained relationship with Marina.

On November 22, 1963, Oswald changed the course of history when he was accused of shooting and killing President John F. Kennedy in Dallas, Texas, from the sixth floor of the Texas School Book Depository. Kennedy's assassination came as a shock to the entire world, and Oswald's actions that day made him an infamous historical figure.

Just two days after the assassination, while being transported by police, Oswald was killed by Jack Ruby, a Dallas businessman, in front of live television cameras, sparking numerous conspiracy theories about his true motivation and whether he acted alone or as part of a larger plot.

Over the years, Oswald's exact motives for defecting to the Soviet Union and then returning to the United States remain a matter of debate. Some believe his defection was a product of his growing disillusionment with American politics and his idealization of communism, while others suggest it was an act of desperation and mental instability.

As for the Kennedy assassination, official investigations, such as the Warren Report, concluded that Oswald acted alone. However, due to his history as a defector and connections to the Soviet Union and Cuba, theories have emerged suggesting the possible involvement of these governments or even the mafia, CIA, or FBI. None of these theories have been conclusively proven.

14. Omar Cabezas Lacayo: From Sandinista guerrilla to regime defector

Omar Cabezas Lacayo is an emblematic figure of the Sandinista Revolution in Nicaragua and one of the most notable defectors from the regime he helped establish. Known for his literary work and revolutionary activism, Cabezas went from being a key fighter against the Anastasio Somoza dictatorship to a critic of the Sandinistas in power, which led to his later defection.

Omar Cabezas was born on January 5, 1950, in León, Nicaragua. From a young age, he showed an inclination towards politics and social struggle, influenced by the poverty and inequalities he observed in his country. In his youth, he joined the Federation of Secondary School Students (FES), an organization that defended student rights and sought to improve access to education in Nicaragua. This was his first approach to political activism.

Later, during his university studies at the National Autonomous University of Nicaragua (UNAN), in León, Cabezas joined the Sandinista National Liberation Front (FSLN), a guerrilla organization that sought to overthrow the Anastasio Somoza dictatorship. It was during these years that Cabezas embraced Marxism and the ideal of armed struggle to achieve social justice in Nicaragua.

In the 1970s, Omar Cabezas became an active fighter in the Sandinista guerrilla. He participated in numerous military operations against the Somoza forces, facing harsh conditions in the mountains and jungles of Nicaragua. His experience as a guerrilla and his vision of the struggle for freedom were immortalized in his most famous literary work, "The Mountain Is More Than Just a surviving green steppe" (1982), an autobiographical book that narrates his experiences during the revolution.

This book is not only a personal chronicle of the guerrilla war, but it has also become a literary reference to understand the revolutionary spirit and aspirations of a generation of young Nicaraguans who fought to overthrow the dictatorship. Cabezas, with his pen, transmitted the sacrifice, hope, and internal contradictions that marked his participation in the armed struggle.

On July 19, 1979, the FSLN succeeded in overthrowing the Somoza dictatorship, and the Sandinistas took control of the Nicaraguan government. For Omar Cabezas, as for many other revolutionary fighters, this was a moment of triumph, as it meant the end of decades of repression under the Somoza family and hope for a more just future for the people of Nicaragua.

Cabezas assumed several positions in the new Sandinista government. He became a prominent figure in the administration, holding important positions such as Defender of Human Rights in Nicaragua. In addition, he continued his activism, defending revolutionary ideals and the Sandinista project in his first years of government.

However, as the years passed, Omar Cabezas began to distance himself from the FSLN and the government he helped establish. The main reason for his disillusionment was the authoritarian direction taken by the Sandinista government, especially under the leadership of Daniel Ortega, who was consolidating himself as an increasingly autocratic leader. Cabezas criticized the departure from the original principles of the revolution and denounced corruption and human rights violations within the regime.

For Cabezas, Sandinismo in power no longer represented the ideals for which he had fought. What was once a popular and social justice movement was transformed, in his eyes, into a repressive system of government that betrayed the revolution. This led to his eventual defection from the regime in the 2000s when he became an outspoken critic of the Ortega administration.

Omar Cabezas' defection from Sandinismo was not a military act, but an ideological and political one. After years of service to the government, he decided to publicly distance himself from the FSLN and express his opposition to the party's authoritarian drift. In several interviews and writings, Cabezas denounced the concentration of power in the hands of Ortega and his inner circle, as well as the repressive practices against the opposition and civil society.

One of the key moments that symbolized his break with Sandinismo was his resignation from the position of Human Rights Defender in Nicaragua. From then on, Cabezas became a public opponent, although he never abandoned his original Sandinista identity, but rather reinterpreted it in the context of criticism of Ortega.

Cabezas is known for being one of the main chroniclers of the Sandinista revolution. His book "La montaña es algo más que una immense estepa verde" is considered one of the most important literary texts on the guerrilla in Latin America. His literary work is not only political but also has a profound cultural impact, portraying life in the guerrilla and the emotional complexities of armed struggle.

Despite his defection from the FSLN, Cabezas continues to identify as a Sandinista, but he criticizes what he sees as a betrayal of the principles of justice and equity that drove the revolution.

Omar Cabezas is remembered as much for his contribution to the revolutionary struggle as for his courageous criticism of the regime he helped form. Throughout his life, Cabezas has proven himself to be a man of deep convictions, willing to sacrifice his position within the government to defend the ideals he believes in. His defection reflects a broader trend in Latin America, where many revolutionaries face the dilemma of supporting governments that, over time, move away from the principles for which they fought.

His life and literary work remain a source of inspiration for those seeking to understand the complex path of revolutions and the internal betrayals that can arise once power is achieved.

15. Jang Jin-sung: From a poet of the North Korean elite to a defector and critic of the regime

Jang Jin-sung is a North Korean defector who gained notoriety not only for his dramatic escape to South Korea but also for having been one of the privileged writers of the North Korean elite, close to Kim Jong-il's family, before becoming a relentless critic of the North Korean regime. Through his work and his testimonies,

Jang has revealed the secrets of the most hermetic regime in the world.

Jang Jin-sung was born in North Korea in 1971, in a society marked by the rigid hierarchy of the communist regime. From a young age, he showed an extraordinary talent for poetry, which led him to attract the attention of the country's cultural officials. In North Korea, art and literature are propaganda tools used by the regime to consolidate the personality cult of the Kim leaders, and those with outstanding aptitudes, like Jang, were carefully selected and educated to serve these purposes.

Thanks to his literary talent, Jang was admitted to Office 101 of the Propaganda and Agitation Department of the Workers' Party of Korea. This department was responsible for creating content that glorified the supreme leader, and the artists and writers who worked there enjoyed a privileged status. Jang was chosen to write poetry that praised Supreme Leader Kim Jong-il and was granted access to certain privileges that the rest of the North Korean population could not even imagine.

In addition to being a court poet, Jang Jin-sung also had access to Office 3, which oversaw external propaganda. This department produced fake literature intended to be read outside of North Korea, primarily in South Korea, to influence public opinion in that nation. Jang, due to his high rank, was able to read texts and access foreign information, which was crucial to his future defection.

Although Jang enjoyed a relatively comfortable life within the North Korean elite, his perception of the regime began to change as he became aware of the huge contradictions between propaganda and the reality of the country. Through his access to foreign information, Jang began to question the official narrative that the government imposed on the North Korean people. While senior officials and the Kim family lived in luxury, the rest of the country suffered from overwhelming poverty, especially during the years of the great famine of the 1990s.

One of the most important moments in his process of disillusionment was when, in his role as an official, Jang was sent to a rural region devastated by famine. There he witnessed the suffering of his people, facing a reality opposite the glorious image that the regime tried to project. This emotional and moral shock prompted him to reconsider his loyalty to the system.

The decision to defect from North Korea is an extremely dangerous one, as the regime imposes severe punishments on both defectors and their families. However, in 2004, Jang Jin-sung decided to risk his life to escape. The event that precipitated his escape was the loan of a South Korean magazine to a friend. Possessing and distributing foreign material is a capital offense in North Korea, and when the magazine was lost, Jang knew the only way to avoid execution was to escape.

Jang, along with his friend, undertook a desperate flight to China, the first step many North Korean defectors take before attempting to reach a third country. In China, North Korean defectors are in constant danger, as the Chinese government cooperates with North Korea to repatriate them. If caught, they face torture, forced labor, and even death upon their return.

Jang and his friend managed to evade capture during their passage through China, thanks to the help of a network of activists and organizations that work clandestinely to assist North Korean defectors. Eventually, after a perilous journey, Jang Jin-sung reached South Korea, where he was granted political asylum. His escape was a remarkable achievement, given his high profile in North Korea, which made him a major target for the authorities.

Once in South Korea, Jang Jin-sung established himself as one of the most prominent and vocal defectors criticizing the Pyongyang regime. He published his memoir, "Dear Leader" in 2014, a revealing book that chronicles not only his life as part of the North Korean elite but also his disillusionment with the regime and his risky escape to freedom. In his memoir, Jang offers a unique insider's view of the workings of the North Korean regime's propaganda apparatus and the cult of personality surrounding the Kim leadership.

In addition to his memoirs, Jang founded a website called New Focus International, a platform dedicated to exposing the realities of life under the North Korean regime and disseminating news and analysis about the country from a critical perspective.

Jang Jin-sung is today one of the most influential critics of the North Korean regime, and his testimony has been instrumental in shedding light on life in the North Korean elite and the country's power structures. His defection was not only an act of personal courage but also opened a window into one of the most closed and opaque regimes in the world.

Jang has left an indelible mark both in the literary field and in human rights activism. His life and work are a testament to the courage of those who risk everything for freedom, and his legacy continues to inspire other defectors and those fighting for the truth in North Korea.

16. Aleksandr Litvinenko: From Russian Secret Service to Kremlin Critic

Aleksandr Litvinenko was a Russian defector who rose from being a high-ranking officer in Russia's Federal Security Service (FSB), the successor agency to the KGB, to an outspoken critic of the Russian government and President Vladimir Putin. His defection and eventual death by poisoning in the United Kingdom in 2006 sparked an international controversy that exposed the ruthless methods of the Russian security apparatus against its opponents.

Aleksandr Litvinenko was born on August 30, 1962, in Voronezh, Russia, when the country was part of the Soviet Union. After graduating from military school, he began his career in the KGB, the main Soviet intelligence service, in 1986. With the dissolution of the Soviet Union in 1991, Litvinenko continued his service in the newly formed FSB, Russia's main internal security agency, where he rose rapidly due to his proficiency in counterterrorism operations.

During his time in the FSB, Litvinenko was assigned to fight organized crime in Russia, one of the most challenging assignments due to the breakdown of law and order that followed the end of the Soviet era. Throughout his career, he witnessed widespread corruption in Russian power structures and links between top officials and criminal groups.

In 1998, while still working for the FSB, Litvinenko was called to participate in a covert operation ordered by his superiors. Instead of a regular mission, however, he was instructed to assassinate Boris Berezovsky, an influential Russian businessman who was, at the time, an ally of Putin but who over time became one of his fiercest critics. Litvinenko was horrified by the nature of the order and, rather than carrying it out, decided to make the information public.

Along with other FSB officers, Litvinenko held a press conference in 1998, in which he publicly denounced corruption within the agency and revealed the existence of illegal assassination orders. This denunciation put him in the crosshairs of his superiors and, above all, of Vladimir Putin, who at the time headed the FSB and would soon become president of Russia. Following his denunciation, Litvinenko was arrested and briefly imprisoned on fabricated charges but managed to be released thanks to the intervention of allies within the Russian judicial system.

Realizing that his life was in danger in Russia because he clashed with the Kremlin, Litvinenko decided to defect. In 2000, he and his family escaped Russia, fleeing to Turkey first and then requesting political asylum in the United Kingdom, where he was accepted.

Once in London, Litvinenko became an outspoken critic of Putin's government. He was protected by his former friend, Boris Berezovsky, who had also fled Russia because of his conflict with Putin. Litvinenko published several books and articles exposing what he described as the corrupt and criminal character of the Russian regime. In his most famous book, "Blowing Up Russia: Terror from Within," Litvinenko accused the FSB of being behind the 1999 apartment bombings in Russia, which served as a pretext for the second Chechen war and consolidated Putin's power.

Litvinenko was also one of the first voices to directly accuse Putin of involvement in criminal activities, including the murder of critics and political opponents. According to him, the Russian government not only used brutal methods against its internal enemies but was also willing to carry out illegal operations abroad.

During his time in the UK, Litvinenko worked with MI6, the British intelligence service, and other Western services, providing information on the activities of the FSB and the Russian mafia in Europe. However, his open opposition to Putin and his accusations made him a priority target of the Kremlin.

On 1 November 2006, Litvinenko met with two former FSB agents, Andrei Lugovoi and Dmitry Kovtun, in a London hotel. During this meeting, Litvinenko was poisoned with polonium-210, an extremely toxic radioactive substance. The poisoning was not immediately apparent, but in the following days, Litvinenko began to suffer severe symptoms, including hair loss, intense nausea, and abdominal pain.

As his health condition worsened, doctors in London discovered that he had been exposed to a lethal dose of radioactivity, which left him seriously ill and eventually led to his death on November 23, 2006. Before he passed away, Litvinenko explicitly accused Putin of ordering his assassination. On his deathbed, he dictated a statement blaming the Russian president for his poisoning and warning the world about the dangers of the Russian regime.

The investigation into his death led the British government to identify Lugovoi and Kovtun as the prime suspects in the murder. Both quickly returned to Russia after the incident, and although British authorities issued arrest warrants, the Russian government refused to extradite them. Lugovoi was later elected to the Russian Parliament and decorated for his "service to the nation," which many interpreted as a sign of the Kremlin's complicity.

Litvinenko's death was the first documented case of an assassination carried out using polonium-210, and its impact was significant globally. Tensions between Britain and Russia rose, and the incident was seen as a clear example of how the Kremlin did not hesitate to pursue its enemies beyond Russia's borders. The nature of the poisoning, so complex and costly, showed that the attack was meticulously planned and that the perpetrators had the backing of the Russian state.

Litvinenko became a symbol of the repression of dissent under Putin's rule, and his case remains one of the most notorious examples of the dangers faced by defectors and critics of the Russian regime. His death also sparked increased scrutiny over the tactics of the Russian intelligence services and their international reach.

17. Shin Dong-hyuk: The defector who escaped North Korea's hell

Shin Dong-hyuk is the only known North Korean defector to have escaped from a North Korean political prisoner camp. His story, told in the book "Escape from Camp 14," is one of the most powerful and moving accounts of the North Korean regime's brutality and the fight for freedom. Born and raised inside a prison camp, his life was marked by repression, violence, and despair. Yet, he managed the seemingly impossible: escaping from one of the most ruthless places on the planet.

Shin Dong-hyuk was born Shin in Geun on November 19, 1982, in Camp 14, an infamous forced labor camp located in the northeast of North Korea. The camp was meant to house political prisoners and their families, under the rule of "guilt by association," a multi-generational punishment in which the descendants of someone deemed a traitor to the regime are also punished. This meant that Shin was considered guilty from birth, without having committed any crime.

His mother, Jang Hye-kyung, and father, Shin Gyung-sub, were prisoners in the camp because relatives of his father had tried to flee to South Korea years before. As was common in these camps, his parents were not a couple in the traditional sense; they were forced to marry by the camp authorities as part of a "reward" program for obedient prisoners. Shin was taught from a young age that his only loyalty should be to the guards and the regime and that any attempt at disobedience meant death.

Life at Camp 14 was a constant nightmare. Shin grew up seeing public executions, torture, and suffering. He knew no concepts like love, freedom, or family in the conventional sense. From a very early age, he was taught to report any suspicious behavior from other prisoners, including his own family, and was indoctrinated to blindly obey the guards. Hunger was constant, and prisoners, including children, were forced to work grueling hours in inhumane conditions.

One of the most tragic episodes of his life occurred when he was 14. After overhearing his mother and brother discussing a plan to escape, Shin reported them to the guards in the hope of receiving a reward in the form of food. As a result, his mother was publicly executed, and his older brother was tortured and killed. Shin was forced to witness his mother's execution, an event that marked him deeply. Years later, he revealed that at that time he felt no love for his family, only fear and an obsession with survival.

For the next few years, Shin continued to live in appalling conditions, until in 2004, when he was 22, he met a new prisoner named Park Yong-chul, who had lived in the outside world before being imprisoned. Park told him stories of life outside North Korea, of the abundant food supply and the freedom that existed in other countries. It was the first time Shin had heard anything about the world beyond the camp, and these stories sparked in him a desire to escape.

Driven by hunger and desperation, Shin and Park decided to plan an escape from the camp. On January 2, 2005, while working in the area next to the electrified fence, he decided to risk everything. Park tried to cross first but was electrocuted. Despite having witnessed his comrade's death, Shin saw this moment as his only chance. Using Park's body to shield him from the current, he climbed over the electrified fence and escaped from Camp 14. After escaping the camp, Shin began a grueling trek on foot to China. He had to steal food and take shelter wherever he could to avoid detection by North Korean authorities. Along the way, he faced the danger of being captured and executed, as would happen to many defectors. After months of traveling through North Korea, he managed to cross the border into China.

In China, he found support from smuggling networks and sympathizers, and eventually made it to the South Korean embassy in Beijing. From there, he was taken to South Korea, where he was granted political asylum and began to rebuild his life. In South Korea, he adopted the name Shin Dong-hyuk and for the first time began to experience freedom, although he also had to deal with trauma and guilt over having denounced his mother and witnessed her execution.

In 2010, Shin became internationally known after the publication of the book "Escape from Camp 14", written by American journalist Blaine Harden. In the book, Shin recounted his experience in Camp 14 and his incredible escape. His testimony shook the world's conscience and put a human face on the suffering inflicted by the regime of Kim Jong-il and Kim Jong-un.

Shin became a human rights activist, dedicated to exposing the systematic violations of human rights in North Korea. He testified before several international bodies, including the United Nations, where his testimony helped prompt the creation of an international commission that investigated the crimes of the North Korean regime. The UN Commission of Inquiry on North Korea called the prison camps crimes against humanity.

In 2015, controversy arose when Shin revealed that some details of his original account were not entirely accurate. He admitted that he had spent time in Camp 18, not just Camp 14, and that he had been moved between the camps throughout his life. This revelation led to criticism and doubts about the full veracity of his story, although the central facts of his escape and the atrocities he witnessed in the prison camps were not questioned.

Shin explained that the inaccuracies were due to the emotional and psychological trauma he had suffered and that he feared being discredited or not believed. Despite the controversies, his story remains one of the most shocking accounts of the brutality of the North Korean system.

Shin Dong-hyuk is a symbol of the fight for freedom in one of the most repressive regimes in the world. His story not only exposes the horrors of North Korea but also the incredible human capacity for survival in the face of extreme oppression. Despite the hardships and criticism, his testimony has helped raise awareness around the world about the reality of North Korean prison camps and the systematic violations of human rights in that country.

Shin remains an activist, although he has expressed that living with the trauma of his past is a constant challenge. His testimony, however, continues to be a powerful voice denouncing the atrocities of the North Korean regime, and his courage to escape the hell of the prison camps continues to inspire those fighting for justice and human rights.

18. Suad al-Shammari: The Defector Who Raised Her Voice for Women's Rights in Saudi Arabia

Suad al-Shammari is a prominent Saudi activist and feminist who fought tirelessly for women's rights in her home country of Saudi Arabia. Suad gained notoriety for her work with the Saudi Human Rights Movement and her association with Raif Badawi, a well-known blogger imprisoned for his criticism of the Saudi government. Eventually, after facing intense persecution and imprisonment for her activities, Suad decided to defect to the United States, where she continued her fight for equality and human rights from exile.

Suad al-Shammari was born in Saudi Arabia, a country known for its strict interpretation of Sharia law and its male guardianship system, which severely limits women's rights and autonomy. Despite growing up in a patriarchal society, Suad always displayed a progressive mindset and a strong will to challenge the injustices she saw around her.

She studied social work and psychology, which allowed her to delve deeper into the analysis of social problems faced by Saudi women. Gradually, Suad began to get involved in the fight for women's rights, openly challenging Saudi laws that restrict female freedom. In 2007, she founded a human rights group together with blogger Raif Badawi, who was arrested and sentenced to 10 years in prison and 1,000 lashes for "insulting Islam." This internationally known case had a huge impact on Suad's life and cemented her as an important figure in Saudi activism.

One of the central points of Suad's fight was the abolition of the male guardianship system, which required Saudi women to obtain permission from a male guardian to carry out everyday activities, such as traveling, working, getting married, or even receiving medical care. Suad became one of the most fiercely public critics of this system, using social media and interviews to voice her discontent and expose injustices internationally.

Through her activism, Suad encouraged Saudi women to demand their freedom, challenging the role traditionally assigned to them in society. She organized online campaigns and spoke at conferences, attracting both the support of reformists and the hatred of the more conservative sectors of Saudi Arabia.

Suad al-Shammari's activism did not go unnoticed by the Saudi government. In 2014, she was arrested and imprisoned on charges of "inciting public disorder and disobeying authority." This arrest was largely motivated by her outspoken criticism of the guardianship system and her support for women's right to drive, which at the time was still banned in Saudi Arabia.

During her imprisonment, Suad experienced firsthand the brutality of the Saudi justice system. However, her arrest sparked a wave of international protests from human rights organizations demanding her release. After spending several months in prison, she was released on the condition that she stop participating in "anti-government" activities. Nevertheless, Suad continued her fight from the shadows, knowing that her life was in danger.

In 2017, fearing arrest again and facing increasing danger to her life, Suad al-Shammari decided to flee Saudi Arabia. She took advantage of an opportunity to travel to the United States, where she requested political asylum. This decision to defect was motivated not only by the persecution she faced in her country but also by her desire to continue fighting for women's rights without the constant restrictions and threats of the Saudi regime.

Once in the United States, Suad continued her activism from exile. She took advantage of international media platforms to denounce human rights violations in Saudi Arabia, especially those related to the oppression of women. She has also worked alongside other human rights organizations to pressure the Saudi government on its treatment of dissidents and activists within the country.

Suad al-Shammari's story has had a significant impact both inside and outside Saudi Arabia. Although she was one of the most prominent voices in her country for gender equality, her activism has resonated internationally, exposing the injustices of Saudi women to the world. Her struggle has contributed to the opening of a global debate on women's rights in conservative Islamic countries and has served as an inspiration to many activists in the region.

Since her defection, Suad has continued to use her voice to demand profound changes to the Saudi system, participating in international forums and remaining active in the defence of human rights. Despite being far from her home country, her influence remains strong, and she is considered an emblematic figure in the fight for equality in the Arab world.

19. Mohammed Abdullah al-Ahmar. The North Yemen strategist

Mohammed Abdullah al-Ahmar was one of the most influential political figures in Yemen during the second half of the 20th century. He was born in 1933 in the Hashid tribal region of northern Yemen to a prominent family traditionally aligned with the resistance of tribal forces against the Ottomans and later with nationalist movements. He grew up in a context of tribal strife, tensions between factions in northern and southern Yemen, and foreign influences in the region. His political career was marked by his relationship with tribal power, Islamism, and the growing conflict between internal and external forces.

Al-Ahmar was elected head of the powerful Hashid tribal clan, which played a crucial role in the country's political struggles. Although he initially supported nationalist and pan-Arab causes along the lines of Egyptian leader Gamal Abdel Nasser, al-Ahmar soon became involved in the Yemeni Revolution of 1962, which overthrew the Mutawakkilite kingdom in the north and established the Yemen Arab Republic. His backing of the republic positioned him as a key leader in North Yemeni politics.

Despite his nationalist and pan-Arab beginnings, over time al-Ahmar began to feel that Egyptian influence and the growing socialist movements in southern Yemen (South Yemen, under Marxist control) threatened traditional tribal and Islamic power structures in the north. In 1970, after several years of conflict, al-Ahmar broke his alliance with progressive forces and allied himself with Saudi Arabia, a country that maintained close ties with the tribes of northern Yemen and supported more conservative and traditional structures. This defection to Saudi Arabia was primarily for strategic and political survival reasons.

Al-Ahmar saw South Yemen as having become a pro-Soviet socialist state and feared that Marxist ideas would cross over to the north, threatening the tribal and religious order. In turn, he considered alliances with Saudi Arabia, a conservative Islamic and monarchical country, to be more in line with the interests of the tribes of northern Yemen. On the other hand, Al-Ahmar rejected Egyptian intervention, as Egyptian nationalists, under the influence of Nasser, played an interventionist role in Yemen, supporting the Yemeni Republic and challenging tribal control. Egypt's withdrawal after its defeat in the Six-Day War (1967) also weakened the position of the Republicans.

Al-Ahmar's shift of allegiance to Saudi Arabia had a significant impact on the politics of Yemen and the region. Al-Ahmar became a key ally of the Saudis, receiving funding and military backing to consolidate his position in northern Yemen. This backing allowed him to establish a strong power base that countered the socialist influence of the South.

Al-Ahmar's defection contributed to the division of Yemen into two blocs: North Yemen, supported by Saudi Arabia and other Gulf monarchies, and South Yemen, aligned with the Soviet Union and the socialist bloc.

Although North Yemen experienced several coups and internal conflicts, the alliance with Saudi Arabia helped stabilize the region in the face of Marxist expansionism from the south. Tribal influence, with Al-Ahmar as one of its most prominent leaders, endured as a central force in the country's politics.

During his political career, al-Ahmar became speaker of Yemen's House of Representatives (1993-2007), consolidating his influence in national politics and actively participating in Yemen's reunification in 1990, when North and South Yemen merged.

Mohammed Abdullah al-Ahmar is remembered as a staunch defender of North Yemen's tribal and religious values and a skilled mediator between the country's rival factions. His defection to Saudi Arabia redefined the balance of power in Yemen for decades, ensuring that the north remained under tribal and Islamic control. His family remains one of the most powerful in Yemeni politics, with his son Sadiq al-Ahmar assuming his role as head of the Hashid clan following his death.

Al-Ahmar died on 29 December 2007, in Jeddah, Saudi Arabia, after receiving medical treatment, and was buried in his homeland as a symbol of his importance to the Yemeni nation.

20. Ali Abdelsoud Mohamed. The Double Face of Betrayal

Ali Mohamed was born in 1952 in Egypt, to a middle-class family. He joined the Egyptian army, where he became a major in the Special Forces. He was trained in military tactics and counterterrorism, which eventually led him to become involved with various Islamic factions. His ability to speak several languages and his deep knowledge of military operations made him a highly skilled figure.

In the early 1980s, Ali Mohamed developed sympathy for radical Islamist groups fighting against Western influences in the Islamic world. At the same time, he began working on covert missions that brought him close to both Western intelligence services and Islamist terrorist networks. His ability to operate in both worlds made him one of his time's most intriguing and dangerous figures.

In 1984, Ali Mohamed was recruited by the CIA while still serving in the Egyptian army. However, his connections to Islamist groups already made him suspect to the Egyptian authorities, who dismissed him from their ranks. After moving to the United States, Mohamed joined the US Army and was assigned to the Fort Bragg base, where he taught Arabic and unconventional warfare techniques to soldiers.

During this time, Mohamed maintained contact with both the CIA and jihadist networks, which allowed him to gain the trust of both sides. Although he officially worked for the US military and intelligence services, he used his position to gather information and pass it on to terrorist organizations, including Al-Qaeda and Hezbollah.

Throughout the 1980s and 1990s, Ali Mohamed worked on planning terrorist attacks for Al-Qaeda, while also providing military training to jihadist fighters. His greatest contribution was his intimate knowledge of intelligence tactics and the vulnerabilities of Western agencies, which he used to train Al-Qaeda members in training camps in Afghanistan and Sudan.

It was Mohamed who helped Osama bin Laden and other Al-Qaeda leaders understand American military intelligence strategies, a factor that contributed significantly to the terrorist network's growth and sophistication. He is also credited with the logistics behind several attacks, including planning the bombings of the US embassies in Kenya and Tanzania in 1998, which left more than 200 people dead.

Although he initially worked for the CIA and the US military, Mohamed was, from his earliest years, a devoted follower of Islamist jihad. His goal was to combat what he perceived as Western occupation of Islamic lands and imperialist control of Middle Eastern governments. Mohamed believed that through his position in the US intelligence services, he could undermine Western efforts and strengthen radical Islamic movements.

Mohamed was a master in the art of manipulation. He knew that working for the CIA and the US military would provide him with access to valuable information that he could use to benefit Al-Qaeda. This "double life" allowed him to move between the two worlds easily, gaining resources and knowledge to help the Jihadist cause.

His departure from Western life was not only ideological but also a reflection of his desire for power and influence within the global Islamist movement. By directly contributing to Al-Qaeda's most important terrorist operations, Mohamed sought a prominent place in the history of global jihad.

The revelation that Mohamed had been working as a double agent for years caused great embarrassment and concern to US intelligence agencies. The fact that someone so close to Al-Qaeda had been able to infiltrate its ranks and the US military revealed serious flaws in the country's security and intelligence systems.

In 1998, Ali Mohamed was arrested in the United States and charged with his involvement in the embassy bombings. Unlike other Al-Qaeda operatives, Mohamed agreed to cooperate with US authorities. However, his case was handled with extreme secrecy, and he pleaded guilty to several terrorism-related charges. Despite his cooperation, he was never publicly sentenced, and his fate remains largely unknown.

Ali Mohamed left a dark legacy as one of the modern world's most notorious double agents. His ability to infiltrate Western intelligence agencies while simultaneously working for one of the world's deadliest terrorist groups made him a feared and hated figure. Although many of his operational achievements were suppressed, his story revealed the depths of the covert war between intelligence agencies and terrorist networks.

His life demonstrated how ideology, opportunity, and personal ambition can converge into a figure capable of challenging world powers from within. Ali Mohamed is remembered as one of the most shocking traitors in modern history, whose actions helped transform Al-Qaeda into a global threat.

✝

Other books by the author Phillips Tahuer that you will find on this platform:

• The greatest conspiracy theories

• Great robberies in history

• Famous murderers - the perverse side of the mind-

• Lives in captivity - Stories of real kidnappings-

• Agents, informants, and traitors - the world of espionage-

• Pirates of the 21st century

• Tragic loves

• 30 curiosities of World War II

• Dark experiments on humans

• Real-life heroes

• Powerful men in modern history

• Valentine's Day stories

• Practical Psychology Lessons